I0758721
This Book Belongs To

祈年殿

中华人民共和国万岁
世界人民大团结万岁

黃鶴樓

T. ZEUS·ATHENS·

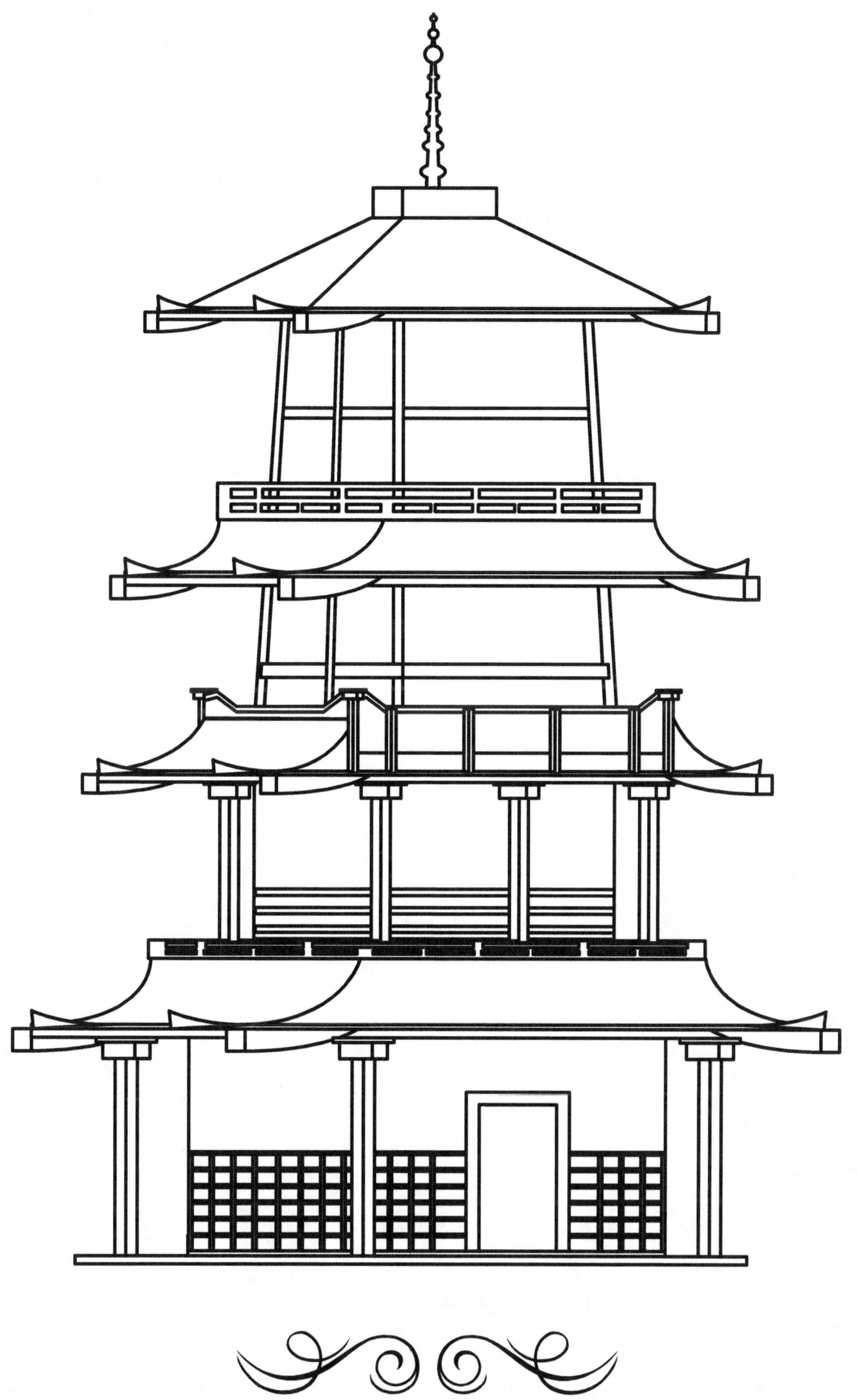

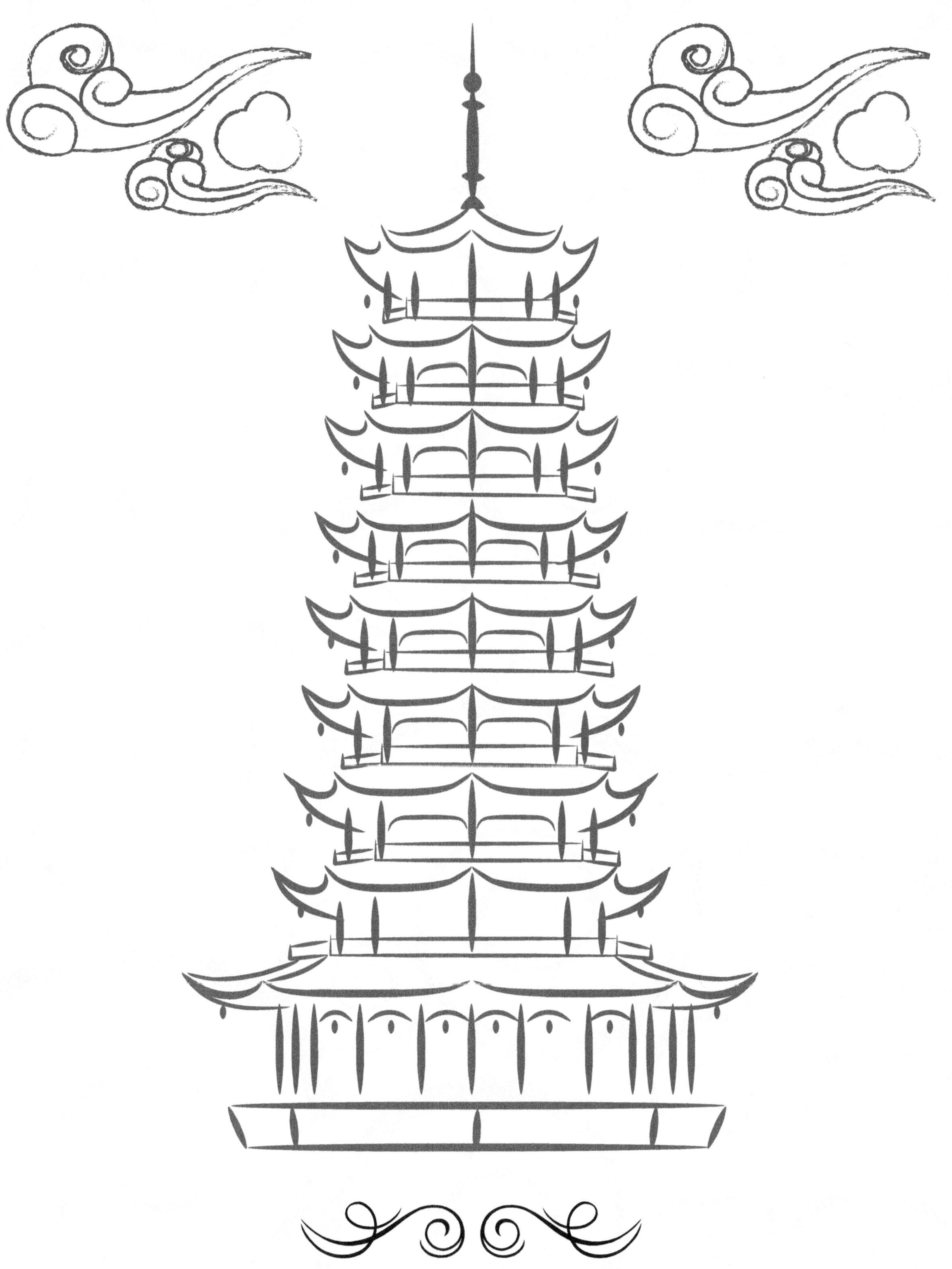

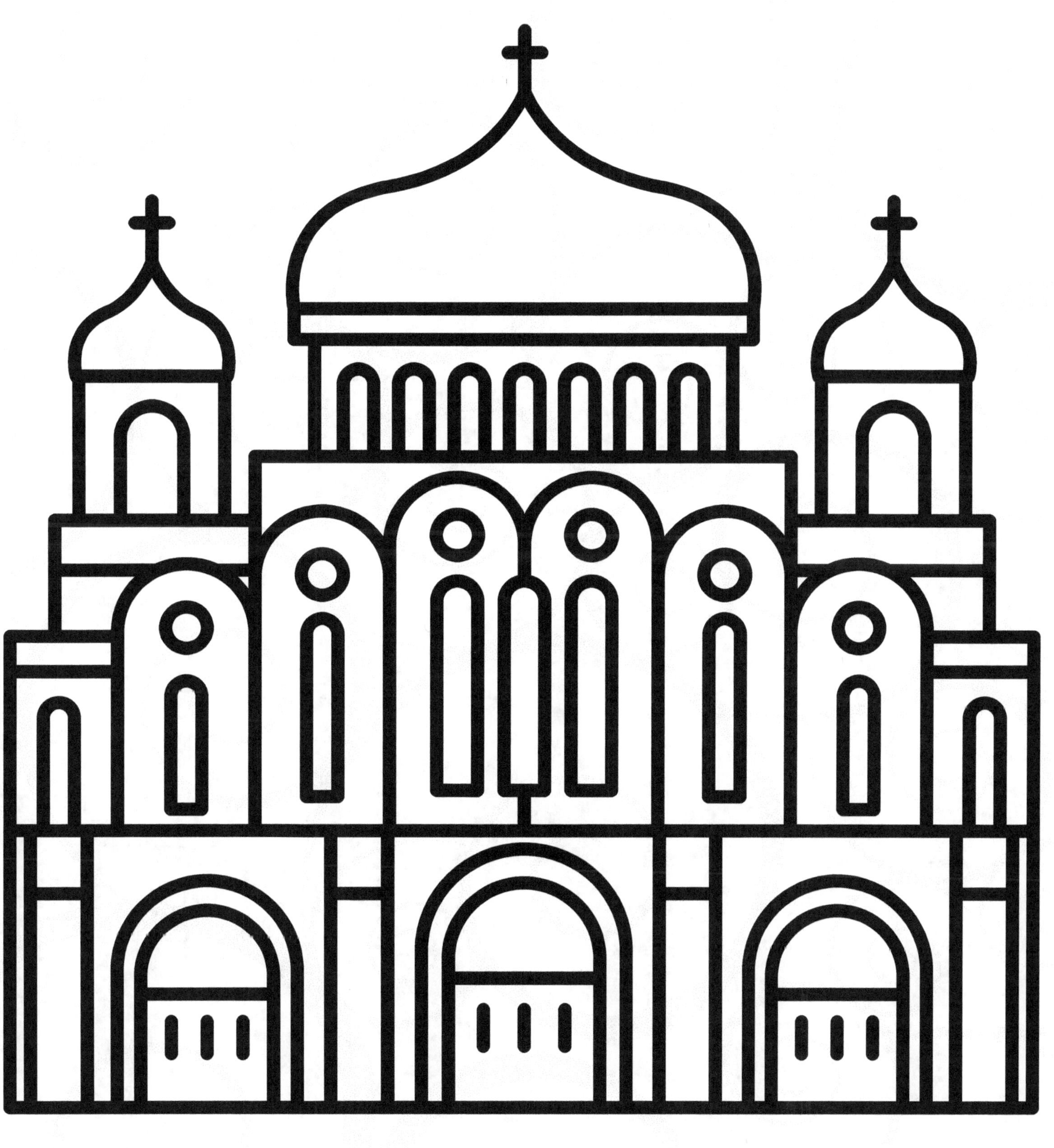

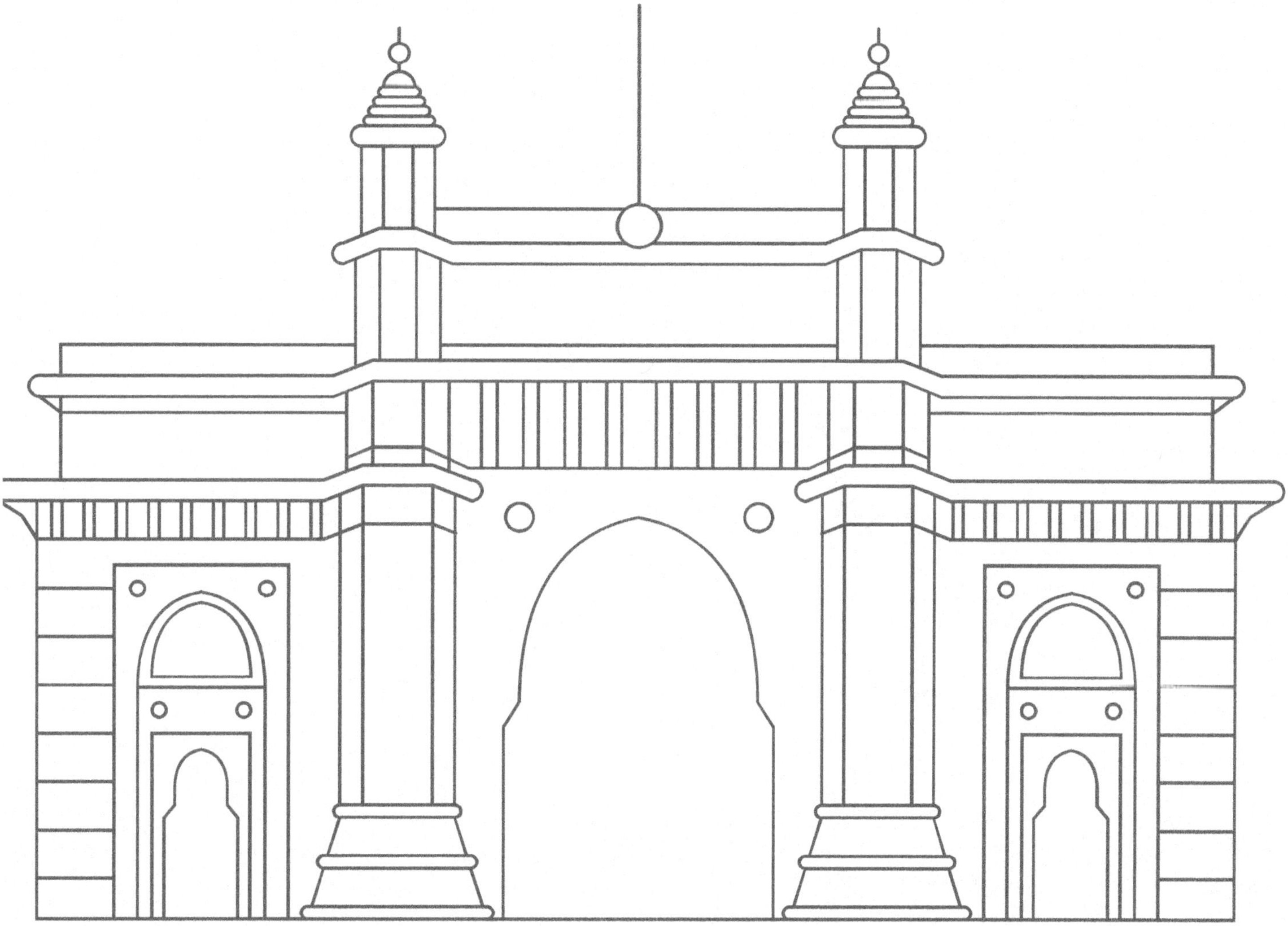

GATEWAY OF INDIA

HAJI ALI DARGAH

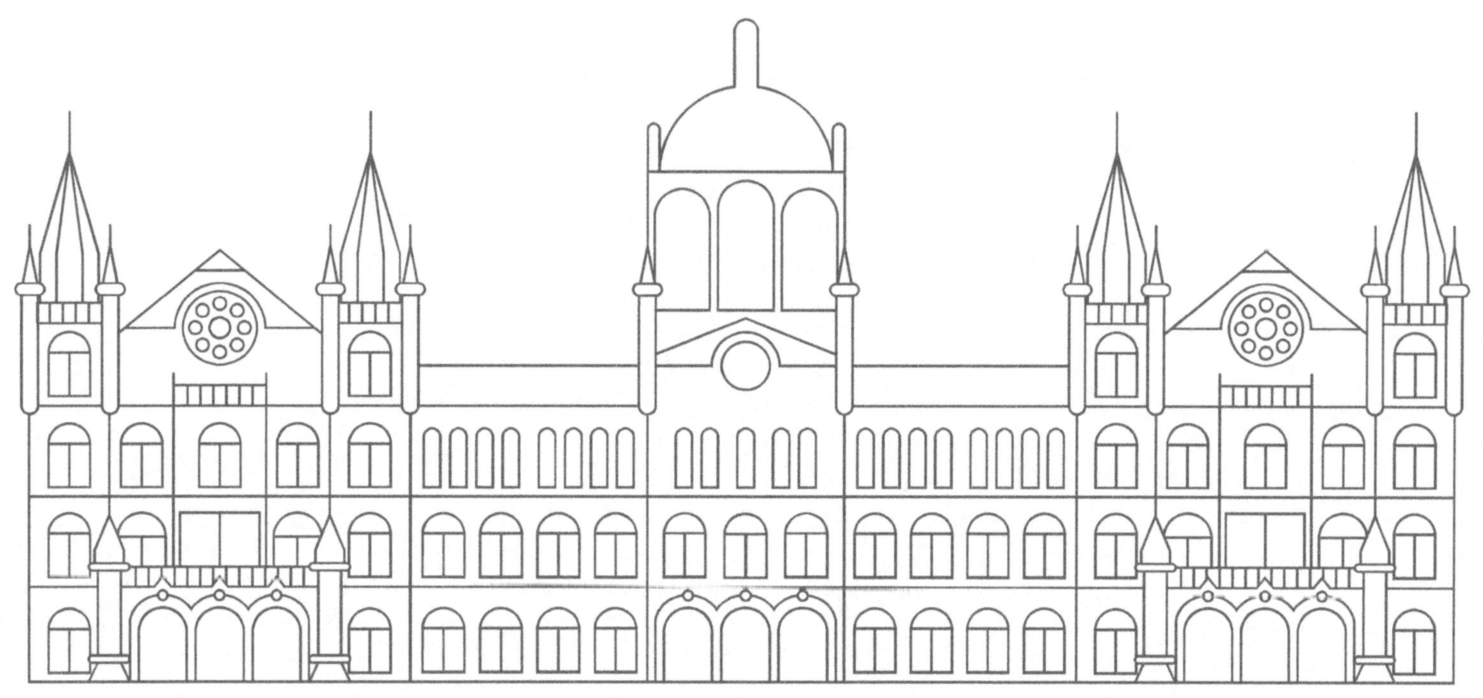

CHHATRAPATI SHIVAJI TERMINUS

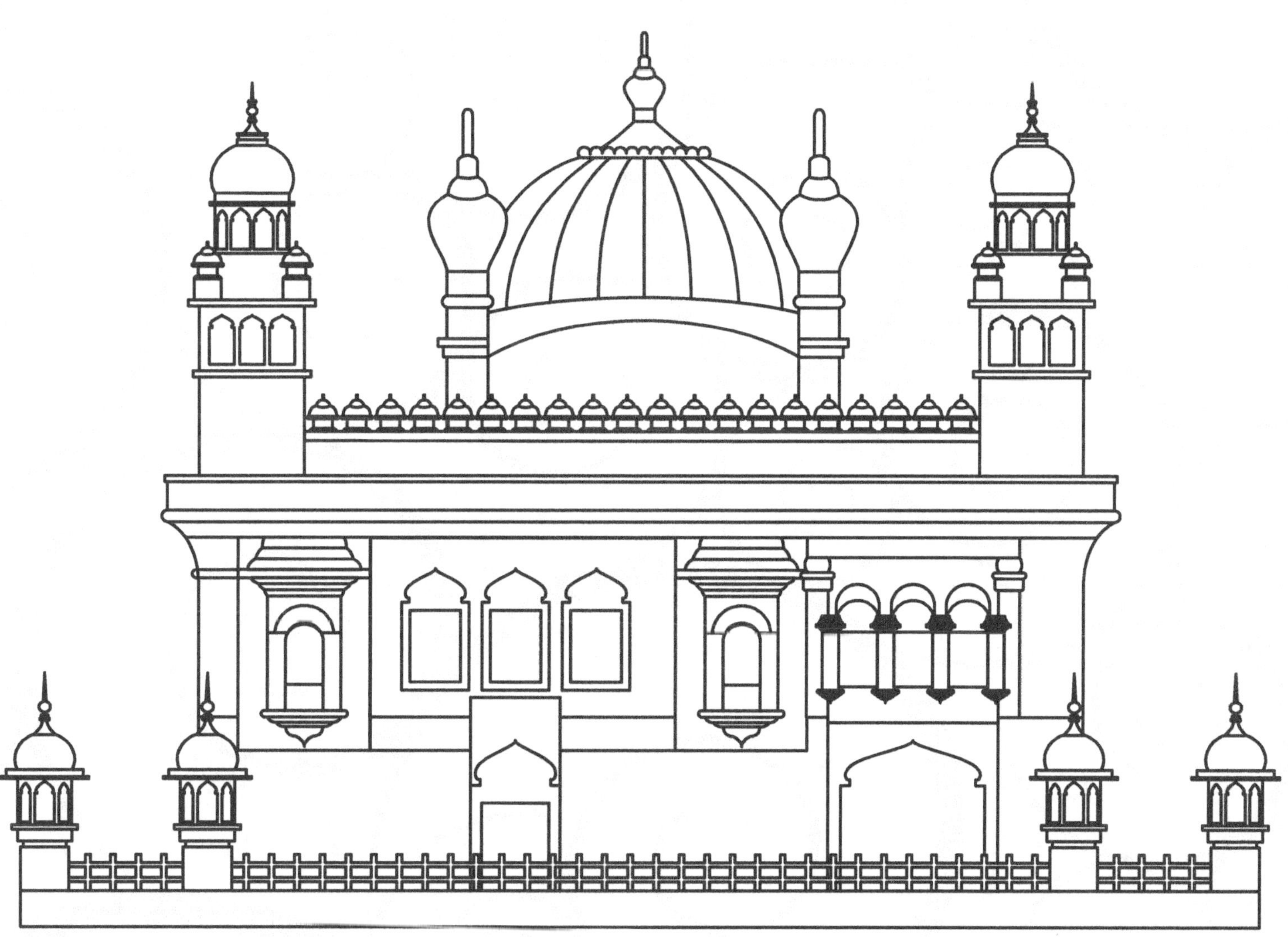

The City Of Prague

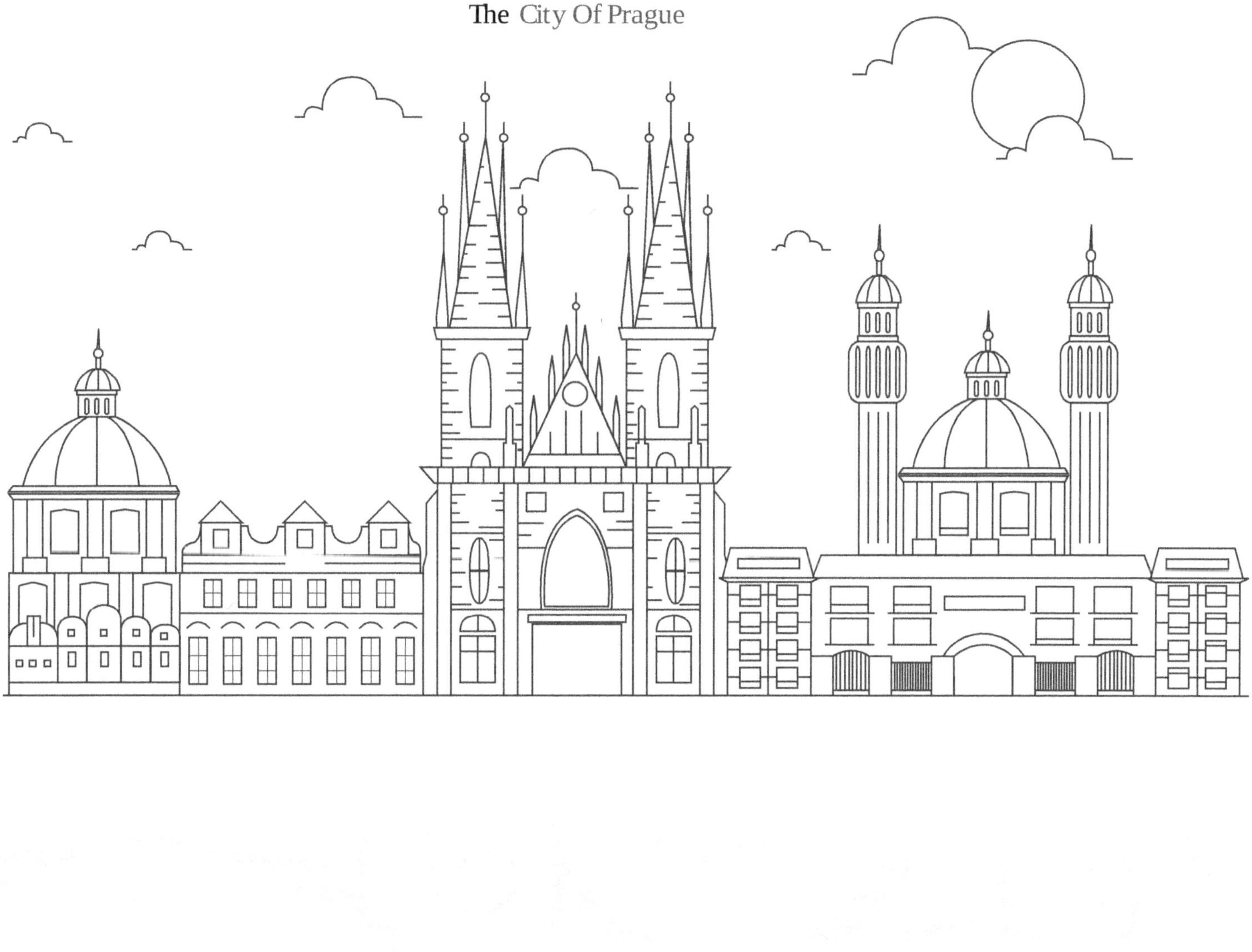

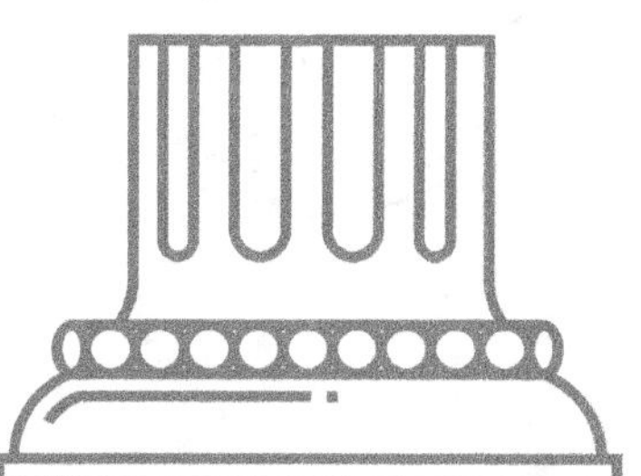
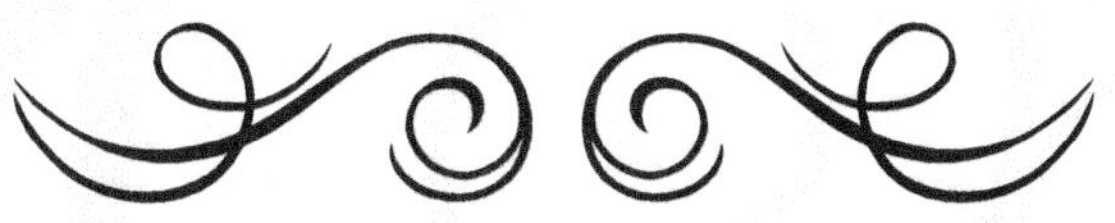

www.ingramcontent.com/pod-product-compliance
Lightning Source LLC
Chambersburg PA
CBHW080225260726
48658CB00008B/3006